The 20th Century's

Most Influential

HISPANICS

Julia Alvarez

Novelist and Poet

Other titles in The 20th Century's Most Influential Hispanics series include:

Roberto Clemente: Baseball Hall of Famer
Che Guevara: Firebrand Revolutionary
Dolores Huerta: United Farm Workers Cofounder
Frida Kahlo: Painter
Jennifer Lopez: Entertainer
Gabriel García Márquez: Nobel Prize–Winning Author
Rigoberta Menchú: Indian Rights Activist
Ellen Ochoa: First Female Hispanic Astronaut
Pelé: Soccer Superstar
Diego Rivera: Muralist
Carlos Santana: Legendary Guitarist

Julia Alvarez
Novelist and Poet

by Clarissa Aykroyd

LUCENT BOOKS
A part of Gale, Cengage Learning

Detroit • New York • San Francisco • New Haven, Conn • Waterville, Maine • London

© 2008 Gale, a part of Cengage Learning

For more information, contact:
Lucent Books
27500 Drake Rd.
Farmington Hills, MI 48331-3535
Or you can visit our Internet site at gale.cengage.com

LIBRARY OF CONGRESS CATALOGING-IN-PUBLICATION DATA

Aykroyd, Clarissa.
  Julia Alvarez: novelist and poet / by Clarissa Aykroyd.
    p. cm. — (The twentieth century's most influential Hispanics)
  Includes bibliographical references (p.   ) and index.
  ISBN 978-1-4205-0022-6 (hardcover) 1. Alvarez, Julia—Juvenile literature. 2. Poets, American—21st century—Biography—Juvenile literature. 3. Hispanic American women—Biography—Juvenile literature.
  I. Title.
  PS3551.L845Z63 2008
  818'.5409—dc22
                                                                    2007025974

ISBN-10: 1-4205-0022-8

Printed in the United States of America
2 3 4 5 6 7 12 11 10 09 08

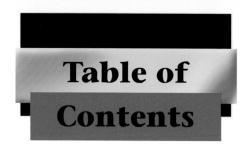

Table of Contents

Foreword

When Alberto Gonzales was a boy living in Texas, he never dreamed he would one day stand next to the president of the United States. Born to poor migrant workers, Gonzales grew up in a two-bedroom house shared by his family of ten. There was no telephone or hot water. Because his parents were too poor to send him to college, Gonzales joined the Air Force, but after two years obtained an appointment to the Air Force Academy and, from there, transferred to Rice University. College was still a time of struggle for Gonzales, who had to sell refreshments in the bleachers during football games to support himself. But he eventually went on to Harvard Law School and rose to prominence in the Texas government. And then one day, decades after rising from his humble beginnings in Texas, he found himself standing next to President George W. Bush at the White House. The president had nominated him to be the nation's first Hispanic attorney general. As he accepted the nomination, Gonzales embraced the president and said, "'Just give me a chance to prove myself'—that is a common prayer for those in my community. Mr. President, thank you for that chance."

Like Gonzales, many Hispanics in America and elsewhere have shed humble beginnings to soar to impressive and previously unreachable heights. In the twenty-first century, influential Hispanic figures can be found worldwide and in all fields of endeavor, including science, politics, education, the arts, sports, religion, and literature. Some accomplishments, like those of musician Carlos Santana or author Alisa Valdes-Rodriguez, have added a much-needed Hispanic voice to the artistic landscape. Others, such as revolutionary Che Guevara or labor leader Dolores Huerta, have spawned international social movements that have enriched the rights of all peoples.

But who exactly is Hispanic? When studying influential Hispanics, it is important to understand what the term actually means. Unlike strictly racial categories like "black" or "Asian," the term "Hispanic" joins a huge swath of people from different countries, religions, and races. The category was first used by the U.S. Census Bureau in 1980 and is used to refer to Spanish-speaking people of any race. Officially, it denotes a person whose ancestry either descends in whole or in part from the people of Spain or from the various peoples of Spanish-speaking Latin America. Often the term "Hispanic" is used synonymously with the term "Latino," but the two actually have slightly different meanings. "Latino" refers only to people from the countries of Latin America, such as Argentina, Brazil, and Venezuela, whether they speak Spanish or Portuguese. Meanwhile, Hispanic refers only to Spanish-speaking peoples but from any Spanish-speaking country, such as Spain, Puerto Rico, or Mexico.

In America, Hispanics are reaching new heights of cultural influence, buying power, and political clout. More than 35 million people identified themselves as Hispanic on the 2000 U.S. census, and there were estimated to be more than 41 million Hispanics in America as of 2006. In the twenty-first century people of Hispanic origin have officially become the nation's largest ethnic minority, outnumbering both blacks and Asians. Hispanics constitute about 13 percent of the nation's total population, and by 2050 their numbers are expected to rise to 102.6 million, at which point they would account for 24 percent of the total population. With growing numbers and expanding influence, Hispanic leaders, artists, politicians, and scientists in America and in other countries are commanding attention like never before.

These unique and fascinating stories are the subjects of The Twentieth Century's Most Influential Hispanics collection from Lucent Books. Each volume in the series critically examines the challenges, accomplishments, and legacy of influential Hispanic figures, many of whom, like Alberto Gonzales, sprang from modest beginnings to achieve groundbreaking goals. The Twentieth Century's Most Influential Hispanics offers vivid narrative, fully documented primary and secondary source quotes, a bibliography, thorough index, and mix of color and black-and-white photographs that enhance each volume and provide excellent starting points for research and discussion.

A Universal Voice

Julia Alvarez, who has published critically acclaimed novels and poetry since the 1980s, has always been inspired by her childhood experiences of moving from one country to another, trying to fit in, and feeling torn between different cultures. She discovered at an early age that writing gave her a feeling of security and personal identity in a very uncertain world. With great determination, she worked for years to develop a unique literary style. Her writing has always incorporated a multicultural perspective—and her first books appeared at a time when such a perspective was less recognized and appreciated than it is now. "With the best and most authentic side of diversity, her voice is a universal one,"[1] comments a reviewer of one of her novels.

Growing up in the Dominican Republic, though born in New York, Julia Alvarez realized that she had a more privileged life than many Dominicans. Still, she dreamed about the United States as an ideal world. When her family moved back to New York, she found that the reality of being an immigrant was exciting but also very difficult. During her teenage years Alvarez discovered that she could escape to another world, that of books and writing.

Surrounded by words, away from the fear of rejection or the possibility of yet another move, she had found a new homeland—perhaps the most important one. She later realized that if she had remained in the Dominican Republic, she might never have become a writer. "When I'm asked what made me a writer," she reveals, "I point to the watershed experience of coming to [the United States]. Not understanding the language, I had to pay close attention to each word—great training for a writer. I also discovered the welcoming world of the imagination and books."[2]

English teachers and other mentors encouraged Alvarez to express herself freely and to read and appreciate the great writers of the past. As a student Alvarez found few role models among

Spectators reach out to touch a portrait of Dominican patron saint Nuestra Señora de Alta Gracia during the Dominican Day Parade in Washington Heights, New York. Growing up in New York, Alvarez tried to bridge her Dominican heritage with her immigrant American identity.

"ethnic" American authors—especially if they were women. "Back then literature by multicultural, ethnic writers was relegated to sociology,"[3] she later said. Alvarez became an important part of a new literary movement, giving a voice to people who had often been silenced: women and racial minorities.

However, Alvarez has never seen herself primarily as a spokesperson for a particular group or movement. She refuses to be placed in a box, resisting being labeled a Dominican writer *or* an American writer. "I shy away from simplistic choices that will leave out an important part of who I am or what my work is about,"[4] she says.

Writing Her Own Identity

The subjects Julia Alvarez chooses for her writing cannot be easily classified or defined. Certain themes appear frequently in her works: Hispanic identity in the American context, the universal challenges faced by women and immigrants, and the struggle to find justice and meaning in an increasingly troubled world. Although her writing often touches on these favorite themes, Alvarez has written on a great variety of topics and in different genres. She has written poetry, nonfiction, and novels, including books for adults and books for younger readers.

Alvarez's first published book, *Homecoming*, is a collection of poems. In it she sensitively explores her own selfhood and that of the women in her family. Her approach is unique and surprising, using subjects such as housework to examine female identity. Her first novel, *How the García Girls Lost Their Accents*, draws on her family's experiences after their arrival in the United States. Later novels treat subjects as diverse as the fight against dictatorship in the Dominican Republic (*In the Time of the Butterflies* and *Before We Were Free*), the distribution of a nineteenth-century vaccine for smallpox (*Saving the World*), and an adopted teenager's search for her roots (*Finding Miracles*).

Alvarez is now best known for her novels, which have received many awards and honors. Despite this, she has often spoken of her special love for poetry, the genre that started her writing career. Poets, she told an interviewer, "are the ones at the cutting edge where language meets the ineffable, the silence."[5]

One of Alvarez's best-loved books is neither a poetry collection nor a novel. *Something to Declare*, a collection of short autobiographical essays, touches on topics such as Alvarez's early years in the United States, her struggle to define herself against her family's expectations, and her choice of Vermont as her "home state."

"Part of La Familia and Also My Own Person"

The writer's lifestyle can be a lonely one. As an author, Alvarez recognizes the need for a certain amount of isolation and contemplation. She has also maintained strong connections to family and friends throughout her writing life. Many members of her extended family did not always understand or approve of her need to write. This was especially true when her work drew on

Traffic jams a street in Santo Domingo, Dominican Republic. Alvarez thinks that moving from the Dominican Republic to the United States as a child made her pay close attention to culture and identity.

aspects of her own upbringing or background. Rifts sometimes developed within the family over her chosen career. Others eventually came to understand that she was not betraying her family but celebrating her origins. Alvarez recalls the supportive words of one of her aunts, and how much they meant to her:

> *Bless you, my daughter. I know how much your writing matters.* The sweetness of both those statements, so rarely put together! Daughter and writer. Part of la familia and also my own person, that full and impossible combination! . . . In bringing me up to belong not just to myself but to la familia, [my family] also taught me to give myself to something bigger than myself.[6]

In the years since she became a well-known author, Alvarez has also benefited from the love and support of her husband, Bill Eichner. Their coffee farm in the Dominican Republic, Alta Gracia, has helped her to maintain ties to her home country and also to give something back. From her home in Vermont to the coffee farm on "the island," Alvarez is now truly Dominican American. She brings that perspective to all of her work. It is only appropriate, therefore, that her life started in the United States, although her earliest memories are of the Dominican Republic.

Chapter 1

The Dominican American Child

Julia was born in New York City, the great city of immigrants, on March 27, 1950. She was the second daughter in a family that would eventually include four girls. Her parents were Dominican, but their backgrounds and the paths that they had chosen in life meant that they were already used to a transient lifestyle. Eduardo Alvarez, her father, was a doctor from a family of little means. In her essay "Grandfather's Blessing," Alvarez recounts that her paternal grandfather, who died before she was born, "left twenty-five legitimate children and who knows how many illegitimate children behind."[7]

Even as a doctor, though, Eduardo Alvarez was not just concerned with helping the sick. His life was governed by strong convictions, including the desire to help free his country from oppression. As a student he had become involved in a movement to overthrow the Dominican Republic's brutal dictator, Rafael Leónidas Trujillo Molina. In 1937, after the attempt to oust Trujillo failed, Eduardo Alvarez fled to Canada. He lived there for nine years before moving to the United States. All the while, he looked forward to the eventual downfall of Trujillo and a return to his native land.

Julia Alvarez was born in New York City (pictured) but moved to the Dominican Republic when she was only three months old.

Julia's mother, Julia Tavares de Alvarez, came from a rich and politically influential family. Julia Tavares's father had studied engineering in the United States at Cornell University, and he spoke nearly flawless English. Julia recalls how her grandfather brought a love of words and a sense of the wide world into her life from an early age. "He loved to recite bits of poetry . . . *Juventud, divino tesoro. How do I love thee? Let me count the ways. Out, out damned spot.*"[8] Her grandfather was a world citizen like no one else she knew. Eventually, he became a cultural attaché to the United Nations, representing the Dominican Republic. Julia's grandparents spent a lot of time in New York, soaking up American culture and mixing with people of various nationalities, and Julia's mother had also spent much time in America. She had been a student at Abbot Academy near Boston, and she too spoke excellent English.

Back to the Dominican Republic

Although American by birth, Julia was not destined to spend her early years in the United States. When she was just three months old, her parents decided to move back to the Dominican Republic. The choice cannot have been an easy one. While the United States was not always a welcoming place for immigrants like the Alvarezes, Trujillo remained in power in the Dominican Republic.

However, Trujillo had apparently decided to liberalize his regime. Unfortunately, after he and his family had returned to the Dominican Republic from New York, Julia's father found "that the liberalization was a hoax staged so that the regime could keep the goodwill and dollars of the United States."[9] Still a ruthless tyrant, Trujillo continued to use the same brutal tactics that had kept him in power for three decades.

Life Under Rafael Trujillo

The Dominican Republic is a beautiful and mountainous Caribbean nation. It shares the island of Hispaniola with another country, Haiti. The American military occupied the Dominican

Generalissimo Rafael L. Trujillo (foreground) inspects his troops in 1959. Alvarez's father became involved in trying to overthrow the brutal dictator.

The Massacre River intersects Haiti and the Dominican Republic. In 1937 Generalissimo Rafael Trujillo ordered the massacre of all Haitians living on the Dominican side of the border. Alvarez's family moved back to the Dominican Republic during this period.

Republic between 1916 and 1924, a period that saw profound changes in the country. During these years an excellent highway system was built, and major improvements were made in areas such as education and sanitation. On the other hand, heavy U.S. and foreign investment meant that native industries were hit hard. In addition, the National Police emerged as an instrument of control and repression, instead of simply maintaining law and order.

In 1930 Trujillo came to power after rising through the ranks of the National Police and the Dominican military. When the former president and vice president went into exile in Puerto Rico, Trujillo became the country's absolute ruler. Over the next thirty years he gained full control of the country's economy and media.

He enforced his rule by terror, organizing a system of informants and dealing harshly with anyone identified as a dissenter.

The horrors of Trujillo's rule also affected neighboring Haiti. Many Haitians lived around the border between the two countries. In 1937 Trujillo ordered the massacre of all Haitians living on the Dominican side of the border. As many as seventeen thousand Haitians died in the massacre.

In his book *Quisqueya,* historian Selden Rodman captures the wickedness of Trujillo's long reign. "The savagery, cynicism, and vulgarity of [the Trujillo dictatorship] filtered from the top down, infecting the whole of Dominican society,"[10] he notes. This was the bleak situation to which the Alvarez family returned in 1950.

A Privileged Childhood

Compared with many Dominicans at the time, however, Julia enjoyed a very privileged upbringing in her native land. Living in the capital of Santo Domingo, surrounded by servants and an adoring family, she was sheltered from the painful realities of life in the Dominican Republic. Her grandfather owned a lot of property, and much of the extended family lived close to each other in houses on his land.

While her father tended to his duties at a local hospital, Julia was brought up mainly by her mother, grandmother, aunts, and maids. "The world was run by women—at least the immediate world I had to live in, which was the only one that mattered to me at that young age,"[11] she recalls. As the main guardians of the children, the female family members and the maids did not have an easy task. The Alvarez girls were not always in good health. One of Julia's sisters had a heart problem and another contracted polio when she was young. Still, the family was fortunate in having access to better food and health care than many other Dominicans.

Julia loved the women who shaped her early years, but she started to realize that they lived in a restrictive world: "Both classes, the maids and the tías [aunts]—I began to see—were circumscribed either by poverty or social restrictions, and both were circumscribed by their gender,"[12] she would later write.

Even in culturally aware families like hers, it was the males who would eventually get a higher education. Daughters were

Alvarez grew up in Santo Domingo and was sheltered from most of the painful realities of life in the Dominican Republic.

expected to grow up to become good wives and mothers. "Reading/studying was not an activity that was encouraged in my family, especially for us girls," she recalls. "My grandmother, who only went up to fourth grade, used to tell the story that she only picked up a book when she heard the teacher's donkey braying as it climbed up the hill to her house."[13]

The Thousand and One Nights

At the same time, storytelling was important in her family and in Dominican culture. Julia was brought up to believe that women knew the tales that made up a family's history more intimately than anyone else. However, they were not supposed to share their private mythology with just anyone—a restriction that she would later have to overcome. She was taught that women were "to keep their mouths shut, to keep things in the family, to be the guardian of the stories and to be very careful who they're released to. It's a way of understanding that stories are powerful."[14]

There were not many books around, especially for the girls, but a maiden aunt had given Julia a copy of *The Thousand and One Nights*. There were suspicions in the family that the aunt had remained unmarried because of her fondness for books. *The Thousand and One Nights* is a collection of medieval Persian, Indian, and Arabic tales. These tales are brought together by a central story involving a strong young woman. Scheherazade, a princess, marries a sultan who has killed all of his wives the day after marrying them. To escape the same fate, she tells him an exciting tale every night and promises to keep doing so as long as he will let her live. Some of the most famous stories from *The Thousand and One Nights* are "Aladdin," "Ali Baba and the Forty Thieves," and "Sinbad the Sailor." These tales of magic lamps, genies, and mysterious lands inspired Julia. However, the best part was reading about Scheherazade, a young woman who used her storytelling

The Power of a Story

When she was a child Julia Alvarez received a copy of *The Thousand and One Nights*, a collection of Middle Eastern tales, from an aunt. The central story, about a princess who saved her own life by telling a different tale night after night, inspired Julia. She started to realize just how powerful storytelling could be—and also that women could take control of their own destinies.

The famous female storyteller Scheherazade inspired Alvarez.

abilities to change her life and to gain power over other people. "She was my first muse long before I knew what a muse was,"[15] Alvarez would recall.

Julia and her family did not get to travel to other countries during her childhood in the Dominican Republic. Under Trujillo's dictatorship it was hard to get permission to leave the country. The family took summer vacations in a seaside village called Boca Chica, outside the capital of Santo Domingo. During the long hot days the children, mothers, and female servants played and relaxed on the beach. At night they fell asleep to the gentle sound of the waves. In these moments it felt almost as though they did not live under a frightening and oppressive government.

The American School

Julia's parents believed that it was important for their daughters to learn English and to maintain a connection to the United States. They decided to send the girls to the Carol Morgan School, which was mainly for American children living in the Dominican Republic. This school, in the suburbs of Santo Domingo, was established in the 1930s. Carol Morgan, its founder, was an American missionary. She was also a friend of Julia's grandmother. Today, the Carol Morgan School is still offering children an English-language education based on an American curriculum.

During her early childhood, Julia heard her parents speaking English only when they were discussing something serious that they did not want the children to understand. At the Carol Morgan School, though, Julia and her sisters were supposed to speak English—and only English. If Julia made the mistake of using a Spanish word, she would be met with a frown and a disapproving comment from the teacher.

At school Spanish was viewed as a second-class language, but at home the children continued to speak Spanish most of the time. The two languages got confused to a certain extent, with English words occasionally slipping in among the Spanish. Already, Julia felt that she was being drawn in different directions. Yet she did not identify first and foremost with any particular country or culture. Rather, she considered her family and the stories that she was growing to love the most important things in her life.

Julia knew that her parents hated the dictator Trujillo. She recalls that her mother used Trujillo as the worst of examples: "Whenever we misbehaved, she would use his example as proof that character shows from the very beginning. . . . When my sisters and I cared too much about our appearance, my mother would tell us how Trujillo's vanity knew no bounds."[16]

Of course, the children did not know the full extent of what went on under Trujillo's regime or how involved their father was in the attempts to overthrow the dictator. When Julia reached the age of ten, though, the political situation intruded into all their lives.

Increasing Danger

By 1960 Eduardo Alvarez had become deeply involved in a plot to oust Trujillo. His underground work against the dictatorship placed the Alvarez family in a very dangerous position.

While they were still in the Dominican Republic, Julia and her sisters were unaware of how serious the situation was. "I think my parents really kept a lid on what was going on," she remembers.

> But I sensed a kind of tension and nervousness and I knew that certain things couldn't be talked about. And I remember that whatever we wrote to anybody, the letters were carefully looked at and we had to rewrite them. I thought often it was because of spelling or something like that, but it was my parents' monitoring because there was very bad censorship and a police state surrounding whatever was written, whatever was said.[17]

Julia Alvarez would later discover what was really going on in the months before the family left for the United States. Her father, and by extension the whole family, was under surveillance by

Trujillo's ruthless secret police, the Servicio de Inteligencia Militar (SIM). Black cars appeared around the Alvarez house at night. SIM agents apparently did not know the extent of Eduardo Alvarez's involvement in anti-Trujillo activities, but the surveillance was an extremely ominous development. Julia's parents started to talk about taking a vacation in the United States. They did not tell their daughters that this vacation was likely to last for years, if not forever.

Because the Dominican government did not routinely permit its citizens to leave the country, the Alvarezes needed a pretext for traveling abroad. Julia's father had some influential American friends arrange an opportunity for him to study to be a heart surgeon in the United States—such training could not be obtained in the Dominican Republic—and he requested a two-year visa for himself and his family so that he could accept the heart-surgery fellowship.

Escape to America

When the visas were granted, the Alvarez family wasted no time: Julia's father booked the first available flight to the United States. Their parents had told the girls that the planned "vacation" to the United States was to be kept secret until it became a reality. But, Julia remembers, "I had told our secret to the cousins, the maids, the dog, and the corner candy man."[18]

Until they reached New York, Julia and her sisters believed that the trip was just a vacation. When they discovered that they were in the United States to stay, the children struggled to get used to the idea of life in another country.

Yet they were leaving behind a life of terrible uncertainty in the Dominican Republic. A few months after fleeing their island home, the Alvarez family heard news of the murders of the three Mirabal sisters. These women were among the most important members of the underground movement against Trujillo. They died on a mountain road along with their driver, brutally slain by agents of the dictator. The grief and anger of the Dominican people at the murder of "Las Mariposas" (The Butterflies)—as the Mirabal sisters were called—helped precipitate the assassination of Trujillo on May 30, 1961.

Dictator Rafael Trujillo in 1956. Julia's father, Eduardo Alvarez, was involved in a movement to oust the dictator.

However, the troubles caused by Trujillo's dictatorship did not end immediately with his death, and members of the Alvarez's extended family, as well as their friends, were affected. Julia Alvarez describes what happened after the assassination of Trujillo:

> Some members of the group who assassinated the dictator went to my uncle's house to hide. When they were caught, my uncle was also taken away. My aunt and cousins lived under house arrest for nine months, not knowing if my uncle was dead or alive. He survived, but the members who had hidden in his house were

killed by the dictator's son. These men were very close friends of my family.[19]

At the time, these incidents were difficult for the children to understand. They did not hear the full details until much later. When the Mirabal sisters were murdered, Julia's parents did not let her or her sisters look at the edition of *Time* magazine in which the story was reported.

In Her Father's Footsteps

"Hard work, community service and sacrifice are refrains of her biography, ideals modelled for her early on by her father, who had to remake his life at 45 after fleeing the Trujillo dictatorship in 1960."

—Marcela Valdes, "The Reluctant Celebrity," *Publishers Weekly,* March 27, 2006, p. 2.

The dramatic events of the dying months of Trujillo's dictatorship would later become the inspiration for some of Julia's most powerful writing. In 1960 and the years that followed, though, Julia was far more concerned with the challenges of everyday life in a totally different environment—New York.

New York, New Life

While New York City was home to many immigrants, this did not make the adjustment to American life any easier for Julia and her family. They moved to a neighborhood called Jamaica Estates, in the borough of Queens. Although this was a relatively wealthy area, the standard of living was not what the Alvarez family had been used to. They had just one maid instead of several. Her father worked longer hours than he had worked in the Dominican Republic. "Papi would get up at four in the morning to be at his oficina at six so that the people who were going to la factoría and had to be there at seven-thirty could see el doctor when they were sick," she remembers. "He would go do house calls when he was done. He'd get home at about eight-thirty, nine at night."[20]

The fact that they were almost the only Hispanic people in their area was especially difficult. Most of the family's neighbors were of

German, Italian, or Jewish ancestry. Instead of fitting in, Julia and her sisters suddenly found themselves in a very small minority.

Julia faced prejudice at her new school. Not understanding where the Alvarez girls came from, classmates asked them if they were Spanish or "Porto Rican." Other children were openly cruel, calling them names or even throwing stones at them. "I told myself that one day I would express myself in a way that would make those boys feel bad they had tormented me,"[21] Alvarez later wrote.

Both Hispanic and American

In those early days, language was a barrier. As former students of the Carol Morgan School in the Dominican Republic, Julia and her sisters had learned some English. But their grasp of the language was limited—and it was quite different from what they heard from their peers in New York.

At home the girls were still speaking mostly Spanish. When she was a little older, Julia also spent time with the Hispanic nurses who worked in her father's Brooklyn office. "These young women were the only models I had of what it might be like to be a professional woman and a Latina in this country,"[22] she remembers. The Alvarez family still had very strong connections to the Dominican Republic and to Hispanic culture. In the short term, though, the girls had to learn to speak English like natives—and to accept American culture as their own—if they were going to flourish in their new home.

Moments of Doubt

During her early years in the United States Julia would watch the Miss America competition every year with her family. Although the Alvarez sisters loved to choose their favorite contestants, the fact that very few of the women came from an ethnic background made Julia doubt if she would ever be truly American.

Alvarez remembers going to the opera with her grandfather and watching the Miss America beauty pageant with her family as important experiences of her early years in the United States. She and her sisters longed to look like the girls they saw on television programs. In 1961 Julia took a train to Vermont to attend a French-language summer camp. It was her first visit to the state that would later become her home.

When Julia was in sixth grade an English teacher asked her class to write imaginative stories, which helped Julia develop a love of words. Julia also discovered the joys of libraries after visiting one with her father. Books became a way for her to escape her problems and overcome her homesickness. They created an alternative world. "I discovered that it was a way to enter into a portable homeland that you could carry around in your head," she says. "You didn't have to suffer what was going on around you."[23]

Julia was discovering a new identity. She was not simply a Hispanic American, but a Hispanic American who loved books and the written word.

Chapter 2

Learning Her Craft

When she was thirteen years old Julia left behind the Catholic day schools of her first few years in New York. Her parents sent her to Abbot Academy, the boarding school her mother had attended as a young woman. Julia's three sisters also went to Abbot Academy. In her autobiographical essay "La Gringuita," Alvarez wrote, "Mami managed to get us scholarships to her old boarding school where Good Manners and Tolerance and English Skills were required."[24] Located in Andover, Massachusetts, north of Boston, this school is today part of Phillips Academy Andover.

It was here that she really started to find herself through writing, discovering that it was her greatest passion in life. Two of Alvarez's favorite English teachers introduced her to writers such as William Butler Yeats, the great Irish poet, and Walt Whitman, the American poet who later influenced her own writing. "I was totally taken with Walt Whitman," Alvarez recalls. "He was the most Latino-American voice I ever heard, wonderfully florid and musical, and [he was] a man of expressive gestures to me."[25] Julia's teachers also helped her to overcome her habit of worrying too much about good marks and high achievement. They encouraged her to write creatively on her own time.

Yeats, Whitman, Shakespeare, and the majority of the other writers that Julia explored at Abbot Academy were part of the literary "canon"—the group of writers accepted as representing the highest standard of literature. Most of these writers were male, and they did not come from anything like a Hispanic American background. Julia loved and admired these writers, but something was still missing. "They taught me my craft; they forced me to go outside my own experience and background," she says. "But it was difficult to find or trust my own voice using only these male models."[26]

Alvarez attended the prestigious boarding school Abbot Academy, which is now part of Phillips Academy in Andover, Massachusetts.

Seeking Influences

At Abbot Academy, where Julia Alvarez went to high school, she discovered great writers such as William Butler Yeats and William Shakespeare. Although these writers opened her mind to the extraordinary possibilities of the English language, she felt that something was missing: Most of the writers were men, and few of them were from ethnic backgrounds. As a young Dominican American woman, Alvarez wondered whether there were writers who could speak directly to her own experience.

The Language and Land of Childhood

At Abbot Academy Julia also studied languages—but not Spanish. Since Spanish was her native language, her course advisers insisted that she study French instead. By now Julia and her sisters were speaking mostly English, so the opportunity to study Spanish would have been valuable. Instead, she says, "I lost the capacity to really express myself in my native tongue. It remains a childhood language."[27]

At the same time, Julia's parents were concerned that the loss of their daughters' fluency in Spanish might have more serious consequences. Although the Alvarez girls were now American in many ways, their parents did not want them to lose contact with the Dominican Republic. They started sending their teenage daughters back to the Dominican Republic every summer to stay with the extended family. The girls resisted being assimilated back into the culture they had left as children.

During one summer on "the island," Julia became friends with another Dominican girl who had lived in the United States. Her friend, Alvarez recalled later, "was the first 'hyphenated' person I had ever met whom I considered successful."[28] The two girls had Dominican boyfriends for the summer.

For a while Julia thought that she might be able to move back and forth between the English-speaking and Spanish-speaking worlds. But her Spanish was limited, and her boyfriend did not speak English. In the end she decided that it was unwise for her to get involved with someone who did not speak her new language. In addition to the language barrier, her boyfriend simply had no experience of the world that she now lived in. It was not an easy choice to make, though. Years later she said of her experience as an immigrant: "I think the hardest thing for me was that division that was created which divided me from myself."[29]

College and Conferences

After graduating from Abbot Academy in 1967, Alvarez enrolled at Connecticut College. This small liberal arts college in New London, Connecticut, gave her the opportunity to further explore and develop her passion for writing. At the time, her main interest was poetry. The English department at Connecticut College awarded her the Benjamin T. Marshall Prize for the best poem written by an English student, in both 1968 and 1969.

Alvarez continued to discover writers who inspired her, including William Carlos Williams. She was taken by the fact that this famous American poet had a background similar to hers. Williams's mother came from Puerto Rico and brought Hispanic culture into his life, but he grew up in the United States. Reading poems such as "The Red Wheelbarrow," Alvarez thought that she could hear echoes of Spanish-language phrasing in Williams's distinctive style:

> So much depends
> upon
>
> a red wheel
> barrow
>
> glazed with rain
> water
>
> beside the white
> chickens.[30]

"So much depends" struck a definite chord. "I had heard a similar expression all my life, *todo depende*," she remembers.

"Everything depended on, well, something else. It was our Spanish form of 'maybe.'"[31]

As a two-time winner of the Benjamin T. Marshall Prize, Alvarez was invited to attend the Bread Loaf School of English Writers' Conference in the summer of 1969. The Bread Loaf School of English was part of Middlebury College, Vermont. It offered a variety of English courses in a serene setting near Bread Loaf Mountain in the Green Mountains of Vermont. The Bread Loaf School was established in 1920. One of its most famous associates was Robert Frost, the great American poet, who taught there in the summers for almost forty years.

Although Alvarez had already met teachers and fellow students who loved literature and writing, the conference placed her in a

Alvarez was invited to attend the Bread Loaf School of English Writers' Conference at Middlebury College in 1969.

new and exciting environment. Suddenly, she was surrounded by other writers, who treated her as one of their peers. "I was 19 and it blew my mind," she says. "Here were all these people who were passionate about what I was passionate about, wanted to talk about it, had writing to show to me that I could respond to."[32]

Beginnings at Middlebury

Alvarez's wonderful experience at the Bread Loaf conference led her to transfer to Middlebury College. This was the real beginning of her long association with the state of Vermont. She studied at Middlebury until 1971, when she earned a BA with the highest honors. In the same year, she won the college's Creative Writing Prize. Robert Pack, the founder of Middlebury's creative writing program, was one of her favorite teachers during this time. While Alvarez was there, Pack was the only poet teaching at Middlebury. "His support and encouragement and generosity influenced me,"[33] she recalls.

Traditionally, Alvarez's family in the Dominican Republic would not have placed much emphasis on a higher education for girls. However, things had changed for them when they moved to the United States. "It had been drummed into us: our true green card in America was an education—a high school diploma, a college degree, a teaching certificate,"[34] Alvarez wrote in an essay titled "Goodbye, Ms. Chips."

Alvarez had now gone considerably farther with her education than the cousins of her childhood in the Dominican Republic. Still, she was not sure what to do next. Although she wanted to be a writer, she knew that supporting herself by writing would be very difficult. She returned to New York City and her parents' home, taking a job producing an ecology newsletter for libraries and other businesses. The position did not really interest her. Although Alvarez wondered whether a higher degree in writing was what she really wanted, she thought it would bring her closer to her goal of becoming a writer than her dead-end job in New York.

Becoming a Teacher

In 1973 Alvarez began her graduate studies, enrolling in a creative writing program at Syracuse University. Syracuse, located in upstate New York, offered a highly regarded MFA in creative writing. Only a small number of students could enroll in the program at any given time. This allowed them to work very closely with the department's writers and teachers. Alvarez later mentioned Philip Booth as one of her finest teachers at Syracuse. Booth, an acclaimed poet who had studied with Robert Frost, was a founder of Syracuse's creative writing program.

During her years as a graduate student at Syracuse, Alvarez also took her first steps into the world of teaching. As an assistant instructor, she taught poetry to first-year students. Teaching would later become an important part of Alvarez's life, almost as important to her as writing. At the time, though, she found it difficult. "The heavy weight of performance was on me," she remembers. "After all, we were the M.F.A.-ers, not the serious Ph.D.-ers, and our capability to teach academic subjects was suspect."[35]

In 1974 Alvarez won Syracuse University's Academy of American Poetry Prize. This prestigious award increased her confidence as a writer. It could also have opened more doors to her, in terms of postgraduate studies. Alvarez's father, who had continued to study

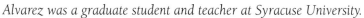

Alvarez was a graduate student and teacher at Syracuse University.

within the medical field and in other areas, encouraged her to get a PhD. Alvarez received her master's degree in creative writing in 1975 and applied to Harvard. Much to her surprise, she was accepted. The university even offered her a fellowship.

But Alvarez did not become a Harvard student. Years later, she explained to an interviewer what happened:

> I didn't turn it down at first. Instead, I went and checked it out. I spent a day attending classes and I thought, "I will die. I will die here." . . . I told [my father], "Papi, I'm going to frame this. On one side you'll have the acceptance letter and on the other side you'll have my letter turning them down. And you can say: not only did I have a daughter who was accepted at Harvard but she refused to go."[36]

Instead of going to Harvard, Alvarez applied successfully for the position of writer-in-residence for the Kentucky Arts Commission. Despite the job's title, it required Alvarez to travel to different towns in Kentucky over a two-year period. In each town she would have a short residency of a few weeks, teaching and reading at schools and colleges.

"Have Typewriter, Will Travel"

By the end of the two-year position, Alvarez had discovered how much she loved teaching, as well as writing. The Kentucky Arts Commission job had not been quite what she expected. Although she spent most of her time teaching in schools, she also worked with prison inmates and with the residents of a retirement home. In one area, Alvarez offered a short literacy class to people who could not read or write. The whole experience proved very satisfying. "Not only did I learn almost everything I needed to know about teaching," she explains, "but I also discovered new authors and texts in my search to find works that might appeal to the different populations I was addressing."[37]

This position set the pattern for Alvarez's life during the next few years. During 1977 and 1978 she held similar jobs in California, Delaware, and North Carolina. In Delaware her workshops led her to edit an anthology called *Yo Soy/I Am*. She edited

Alvarez used to joke that her license plate should have read, "Have Typewriter, Will Travel," because she would travel to any town that would hire her as a writer.

another anthology called *Old Age Ain't for Sissies* after leading poetry workshops for senior citizens in North Carolina.

From 1979 to 1981 Alvarez taught at Phillips Academy Andover in Massachusetts. Her old boarding school, Abbot Academy, had merged with Phillips Academy a few years previously, so the position brought her back to a familiar place. She taught poetry and literature as well as creative writing. She was also an adviser to the school's Afro-American–Latino Society. Alvarez remembers that because she had lived in a half-dozen states over just a few years, "I used to joke that I should get vanity plates that read, HAVE TYPEWRITER, WILL TRAVEL, because I would take a job anywhere that would hire me as its visiting writer."[38]

Maxine Hong Kingston in her Oakland, California, home on April 10, 2001. Her book The Woman Warrior *influenced Alvarez as well as many other Hispanic American writers.*

Finding Herself as a Writer

Although Alvarez appreciated these varied experiences, she felt uncertain about where her life was going. She had sold a few poems to poetry magazines, but she did not yet have any major publications to her name. Alvarez had also experienced problems in her personal life during these years. Before the age of thirty she married twice, but both marriages ended in divorce. Most years she went back to the Dominican Republic to visit her extended family. Her cousins had their own families and a degree of stability in their lives that she envied.

At the same time, Alvarez felt that as a writer she was finally starting to access her own authentic voice. Finally, books by American women from ethnic backgrounds were beginning to be recognized. This helped Alvarez to see that she could follow a similar path. She read *The Woman Warrior* by Maxine Hong Kingston. A memoir about growing up in the United States in a Chinese immigrant family, this book describes experiences that are different from Alvarez's. However, Alvarez related to Kingston's struggle, in *The Woman Warrior* and in later fictional works, to define herself as a woman. The book influenced many other Hispanic American women writers. "So many Latina writers will tell you," Alvarez says, "that [*The Woman Warrior*] was the book that did it."[39]

A turning point in her own writing came in the summer of 1981, when she earned a residency at Yaddo as a fiction writer. An artists' community in Saratoga Springs, New York, Yaddo offers talented musicians, painters, photographers, sculptors, writers, and other creative artists the opportunity to pursue their craft in a tranquil environment. As Alvarez sat in her room at Yaddo and prepared to write, she found an important inspiration. "The voice I heard when I listened to myself think," she recounted in "Of Maids and Other Muses," an autobiographical essay, "was the voice of a woman, sitting in her kitchen, gossiping with a friend over a cup of coffee. . . . And then, hallelujah—I heard the vacuum going up and down the hall. I opened the door and introduced myself to the friendly, sweating woman, wielding her vacuum cleaner."[40]

Alvarez spent some time chatting with the household staff at Yaddo and looking through the cook's favorite book of recipes.

Finding a Voice

At Yaddo, the artists' community in Saratoga Springs, New York, Alvarez began to find her own voice as a writer. As she took the time to find out what subjects were important to her, she also spent time with some of Yaddo's household staff. It was at Yaddo that she started to write the "Housekeeping" poems, which would become the basis for her first poetry collection, *Homecoming*.

She found herself jotting down the names of items in the kitchen, some of which she remembered from her childhood. The vocabulary in the cookbook led her to start a series of poems about housekeeping. Later, these would become the basis of her first poetry collection.

"I Had Gone Public with a Voice"

By 1984 Alvarez had added Vermont to the list of states where she had worked, and she had moved on to a teaching fellowship at George Washington University in Washington, D.C. In that year *Homecoming*, her first collection of poems, was published by Grove Press. Most of the poems in the book had been written in her small apartment in Burlington, Vermont, during her time as a teacher at the University of Vermont.

The experience of seeing her first book in print was both thrilling and somewhat terrifying. Alvarez recalls her conflicting emotions: "What had I done? I had gone public with a voice! I was excited, I was scared, I wasn't sure I shouldn't hide my face until all the books out there were sold and forgotten. . . . I think of that young woman so often when I write. I am still she, heart pounding in my chest, wondering, Do I dare?"[41]

Homecoming includes a series of poems under the collective title "Housekeeping." In many of these poems Alvarez watches her mother working around the house or helps her with the

Alvarez published her first volume of poems while performing a teaching fellowship at George Washington University.

household chores. The poems reflect her love for her mother, but they also show that Alvarez does not want to follow the path expected for a good Dominican woman. The poem "Dusting" illustrates this well:

> She erased my fingerprints
> from the bookshelf and rocker,
> polished mirrors on the desk
> scribbled with my alphabets. . . .
> But I refused with every mark
> to be like her, anonymous.[42]

Homecoming also included a series of sonnets called "33." Alvarez was thirty-three years old when *Homecoming* was published, and this series contains thirty-three poems. In them Alvarez worries about being single, tries not to be lonely, and reflects on the presence of evil in the world.

The Poet Emerges

"Alvarez claims her authority as a poet with this collection."

—Publishers Weekly on *Homecoming*, in Julia Alvarez, *Homecoming: New and Collected Poems.* New York: Plume, 1996, p. i.

Homecoming was well received by critics. One reviewer said: "This is a book in which every woman will recognize the necessities and choices that make up her life."[43] *The Housekeeping Book*, a special edition of the "Housekeeping" poems with illustrations, also appeared in 1984.

Alvarez had now gained a measure of success. Still, a few of her deepest wishes remained unfulfilled. She wanted a more stable life, and she hoped to publish a major work of fiction. In the next few years she would realize these ambitions.

Chapter 3

García Girls and Butterflies

B y the mid-1980s Alvarez had decided that she wanted to devote herself to writing. But because she doubted that she could support herself solely through her writing, she sought a permanent teaching position. She had grown tired of moving from one state to another in pursuit of temporary teaching posts.

"There were times when I thought, how can I write?" she remembers. "Summers were always spent searching for the next job, and moving myself there and starting a new job. And a year after being the 'Visiting This,' I had to move on."[44]

In 1985 Alvarez landed her most important job yet. She became an assistant professor in the English department of the University of Illinois, where she taught until 1988. In addition to teaching literature, poetry, and women's studies, Alvarez acted as a judge for student writing awards. However, her own career remained uncertain. The university had not offered Alvarez the possibility of tenure, or a position as a permanent professor.

Altos de Chavón

During the winter of 1988 Alvarez returned to the Dominican Republic. Instead of visiting her family, she stayed at Altos de

Chavón, an artists' colony, for three months. The village of Altos de Chavón, located about one hundred miles (160km) from the capital of Santo Domingo, was built in 1976 to celebrate the cultural achievements of the Dominican Republic. Its beautiful buildings reflect the architecture of different eras in the country's history. Artists work to produce traditional crafts in the village's workshops, while the amphitheater hosts concerts by major performers. Alvarez was one of five international artists chosen to work at Altos de Chavón in 1988.

As an artist-in-residence at Altos de Chavón, she was able to write in a quiet and beautiful setting, surrounded by the familiar sights and

When Alvarez returned to the Dominican Republic, she continued writing at Altos de Chavón, an artists' colony.

smells of the Dominican Republic. She conducted some workshops and gave readings from her work. Mainly, though, she was writing a book, to which she had not yet been able to devote much time.

"Being so nomadic and having no stability, it was a book that I wrote the way many women write their first books," she says. "So many of them get up at 5 A.M., before the baby gets up. I didn't have that kind of family, but I had those kinds of jobs."[45]

Stability and a *Compañero*

However, Alvarez's nomadic lifestyle was starting to settle down. In 1988 her old school, Middlebury College in Vermont, offered her a tenure-track position. She could become a permanent professor in Middlebury's English department if she continued to teach there and fulfilled certain requirements. One of her teaching assignments was an introductory course in which English students learned how to analyze a wide variety of literary genres. Her major interests, such as Hispanic American literature and women's literature, were reflected in some of the other courses that she taught at Middlebury. Her colleagues also urged Alvarez to keep working toward a major publication, as this would help ensure she was granted tenure.

In 1989 Alvarez made one of the most important decisions of her life. She married Bill Eichner, a doctor from Nebraska. The couple had met in Vermont, and that was where they both wanted to settle. Although he was a doctor, Eichner came from a rural background and loved farming. Alvarez and Eichner decided to build a house on an eleven-acre farm (4.5ha) in Weybridge, Vermont. "At our wedding, we danced on the floor of the unfinished house with friends, many of whom had come from all the areas of the country I had lived in,"[46] Alvarez remembers.

Alvarez often refers to Eichner as her *compañero*—an affectionate Spanish term for the love of her life. Many of her books are dedicated to him. Alvarez writes about Eichner as a steadying influence who has also helped her to see the world in a different light. In one of her autobiographical essays, "Briefly, a Gardener," she writes humorously about her efforts to get interested in her husband's farming and gardening endeavors. "We'll make you a little raised bed," he suggests. This prompts her to think, "Eight years ago when we met in the grocery store . . . I would have

Writing in the Family

Julia Alvarez's third husband, Bill Eichner, is a doctor with a longstanding interest in nutrition and sustainable farming. In 2000 Eichner published a book of his own, *The New Family Cookbook: Recipes for Nourishing Yourself and Those You Love.*

guessed a raised bed is what ex-hippies started to sleep on once they decided to get their mattresses up off the floor."[47]

First Novel

At the age of forty, Alvarez was finally getting close to becoming a recognized author. Although poets and critics had appreciated *Homecoming*, books of poetry do not normally have a wide readership. Alvarez was still writing poetry, but she wanted to bring the stories within her to readers throughout the United States and beyond.

In 1990 she was awarded the Ingram Merrill Foundation Grant, which helped her to complete the manuscript of her first novel. *How the García Girls Lost Their Accents* was published by Algonquin Books of Chapel Hill in 1991. Algonquin, which Alvarez appreciatively calls "a small publisher willing to take a chance on a new voice,"[48] continues to publish her books today.

How the García Girls Lost Their Accents was actually made up of fifteen related stories, all about the same family. Some of the stories had already appeared, in alternate versions, in publications such as the *Caribbean Writer* and the *Syracuse Scholar*. Alvarez dedicated the book to Pack, her creative writing teacher at Middlebury, and to her sisters.

Sisters

Alvarez's first novel drew heavily on her family's experiences when they first arrived in the United States. Alvarez came from a family with four girls, and the sisters in the novel, Carla, Yolanda, Sandra,

Alvarez completed her first novel, How the García Girls Lost Their Accents, *in 1991.*

and Sofía García, have a great deal in common with her and her sisters. When asked if the characters were based on her sisters, Alvarez said: "I certainly come from a family of sisters, so I understand that kind of family dynamic very well."[49]

How the García Girls Lost Their Accents touches on many experiences of sisterhood, from matching outfits to the girls' rebellion against their parents' traditional values. The stories that make up the novel also address the issue of moving from one culture to another and the hardships accompanying this experience. In the story "Daughter of Invention" the girls are frustrated because their parents do not seem to understand the challenges they face as young immigrants from the Dominican Republic: "Why had they come to this country in the first place? Important, crucial, final things, and here was their own mother, who didn't have a second to help them puzzle any of this out."[50]

Extraordinary Women

"By creating fictional characters for the national heroines, Alvarez demythologises them. She brings them back to life not as saints, but as ordinary, yet extraordinary women who respond to oppression out of their personal values and character."

—Ben Jacques, "Julia Alvarez," *Americas*, vol. 53, no. 1, January/February 2001.

The stories do not appear in chronological order. Rather, they start with the sisters as grown women and go backward. Each story explains something about the story before it. Eventually, the book takes its readers back to the sisters' childhood in the Dominican Republic. There, before the family has any idea that its future lies in the United States, the children experience not only disastrous art lessons but also the horror of the Dominican secret police. Throughout the novel, which explores broken relationships, family feuds, and attempts to return to the home country, Alvarez reaffirms the importance of *la familia*, as she calls it.

Many of the elements characteristic of Alvarez's writing style can also be seen in *How the García Girls Lost Their Accents*. The novel features a warm, humorous narrative voice, the use of Spanish words to highlight the characters' roots, and a deep understanding of the problems faced by immigrants and women everywhere.

Alvarez was surprised at how well her novel was received. In general, critics were delighted by *How the García Girls Lost Their Accents*. The *San Diego Tribune* commented, "In a subtle but powerful way it reveals the intricacies of family, the impact of culture and place, and the profound power of language."[51] Another newspaper, the *Washington Post*, said, "Alvarez treats the subjects of immigration, exile, Hispanic culture and the American Dream with a sensitive and often irreverent touch."[52]

Reactions: The Public and La Familia

As Alvarez had hoped, the novel's publication led to her being granted tenure. From 1991 she was a full professor at Middlebury College.

Still, not everyone liked the fact that Alvarez had explored aspects of her own life to write her first novel. Many members of her family had a particularly hard time with the whole idea. Alvarez's mother did not speak to her for months. The publication of such a book was not part of the family's ideas about how their daughters should behave. But not everyone in the family reacted in the same way, remembers Alvarez: "La familia, which had always seemed so monolithic to me, was really quite diverse in its opinions. There were camps among my people. It was one of the advantages of coming from a large, tribal family. A couple of cousins were not talking to me—well, there were at least two dozen who were."[53] A bit later, when the novel had gained more success and recognition, Alvarez's family generally became more accepting of the path that their unconventional daughter had chosen.

How the García Girls Lost Their Accents sold well, and it received several honors. It was awarded the 1991 Pen Oakland/Josephine Miles Award, which recognizes books written from a multicultural perspective. The American Library Association and the *New York Times* Book Review both selected it as a Notable Book.

Alvarez did not try to capitalize on the success of *García Girls* by following up with a second novel on a similar theme. She knew that to develop her art, she needed to explore different subjects. Alvarez also wanted to exorcise a part of her country's history that had haunted her for a long time.

Las Mariposas

Alvarez's research into the Mirabal sisters—"Las Mariposas," or "The Butterflies"—had begun in 1986 on one of her many trips back to the Dominican Republic. However, she had first heard of the Mirabals in 1960, shortly after her family's move to the United States, when she had furtively read a *Time* magazine article about the murder of the sisters.

As young women, Patria, Minerva, María Teresa, and Dedé Mirabal had become involved in the underground movement to overthrow Trujillo's dictatorship. Starting with Minerva, the sisters had relationships with men who were part of the resistance. However, their roles were not simply those of passive supporters. In addition to helping their husbands, the Mirabal sisters became heroines of the underground movement in their own right. They stockpiled ammunition, constructed bombs, and spent months in prison.

On November 25, 1960, Minerva, María Teresa, and Patria were on their way to visit their imprisoned husbands. Dedé, who was not as deeply involved in the movement, was not with them. On a remote mountain road, members of the SIM ambushed the three sisters and murdered them, along with their driver, Rufino de la Cruz. The date of their death has since been commemorated in many Latin American countries as the International Day Against Violence Towards Women.

Alvarez's family had a certain connection to the Mirabal sisters. Although she did not know it at the time, her father was part of the same underground movement. The Alvarezes had left the Dominican Republic because his activities were endangering the whole family. Years later, Julia Alvarez would feel a kind of survivor's guilt. In her essay "Chasing the Butterflies," she wrote, "These three brave sisters and their husbands stood in stark contrast to the self-saving actions of my own family and of other Dominican exiles. Because of this, the Mirabal sisters haunted me."[54]

Finding the Mirabal Sisters

Alvarez's in-depth exploration of the Mirabals' lives started with a minor project. In 1986 a publisher had asked her to write a short

related through entries in her personal diary, including entries during the months that she and Minerva spend in prison. During that difficult time, María Teresa and Minerva find solace in the company of other imprisoned women. "I feel sad to be leaving," writes María Teresa in her last diary entry before they are released. "Yes, strange as it sounds, this has become my home, these girls are like my sisters. I can't imagine the lonely privacy of living without them."[59]

The frame of the story is a 1994 meeting between a Dominican American writer and Dedé. Reluctantly, Dedé is led by the interviewer's curiosity into her memories of her family and the revolutionary struggle. Alvarez also has to describe their deaths and the aftermath in the epilogue because the murdered sisters can no longer tell their own story at that point.

"Alvarez was criticized by some reviewers," one commentator noted, "for relegating the sisters' deaths to a twenty-page epilogue." Yet her "decision not to dwell . . . on their deaths points to the fact that the book serves as a celebration of their lives."[60]

Tears of Joy

Most critics, as well as the novel's many readers, found *In the Time of the Butterflies* deeply moving. Sandra Cisneros, another Latina writer, said: "I was moved to tears, not of sadness but of joy. The sisters Mirabal continue to live as long as women like Julia Alvarez are brave enough to tell their story."[61] The Hispanic author Rudolfo Anaya said in tribute: "It is destined to take its place on the shelf of great Latin-American novels."[62]

Alvarez herself was impressed by the reaction of some readers. Years after the book's publication, she remembers one response:

> One time a reader called me up from California. He was the son of one of the worse torturers in the secret police in the Dominican Republic during the Trujillo regime. He identified himself, said his *mami* had fled to California, leaving his father. She never told him any of the stories. Once he mentioned my novel *In the Time of the Butterflies,* and she told him not to read it. But he was curious and picked up a copy, read it secretly. He

said that at last he understood who his father had been, what he had done. The young man was weeping. I told him that just his reaction was an incredible redemptive sign, that we all carry the dictator and torturer within us. . . . It touched me so much to know that he had pursued the truth, that he was strong enough to face it, fragile enough to let himself feel remorse.[63]

The positive reaction of her family was more important than anything else. Her mother had been dismayed by her first novel,

Author Rudolfo Anaya complimented Alvarez's work, In the Time of the Butterflies.

Author Sandra Cisneros (seen here) was photographed along with Ana Castillo, Denise Chávez, and Julia Alvarez by Vanity Fair *magazine for a profile of Latina writers in 1994.*

Alvarez's novel In the Time of the Butterflies *was made into a movie of the same name starring actress Salma Hayek in 2001.*

which seemed to give away family secrets. This time, Julia Tavares de Alvarez was afraid that a novel about the Mirabal sisters would attract negative attention from surviving members of Trujillo's regime. The book might even endanger their family. After all, Eduardo Alvarez had been part of the resistance movement. However, the response of her mother to the completed novel touched Julia Alvarez deeply:

> I inscribed a copy to both Mami and Papi with a note: "Thank you for having instilled in me through your sufferings a desire for freedom and justice." . . . Days later, my mother called me up to tell me she had just finished the novel. "You put me back in those days. It was like I was reliving it all," she said sobbing. "I don't care what happens to us! I'm so proud of you for writing this book."[64]

In the Time of the Butterflies, like *How the García Girls Lost Their Accents*, was selected as a Notable Book by the American Library Association. A year later, in 1995, the ALA and the Young Adult Library Services Association also chose it as a Best Book for Young Adults, although the novel was not intended for a young adult audience. In 2001 *In the Time of the Butterflies* became a movie, starring Salma Hayek.

"Las Girlfriends"

Alvarez was recognized in a more unexpected way in 1994. Along with the Latina writers Ana Castillo, Denise Chávez, and Sandra Cisneros, she was photographed and interviewed by *Vanity Fair*. All four writers were from the same generation, and they were fans of one another's writing. *Vanity Fair* dubbed them "Las Girlfriends."

The famous magazine suggested that these women were responsible for a new kind of writing, from a background that was both foreign and American. Thinking about the influence of writers such as Maxine Hong Kingston, Alvarez did not really agree. She had mixed feelings about the *Vanity Fair* experience. "We were all a little embarrassed by it," she recalls. "Aware that we were made into a product. There is always that sense of being marketed when they do something like that. But hey, we are still in touch with each other, still reading each other, still girlfriends."[65]

The success of both *García Girls* and *Butterflies* gave Alvarez a new kind of freedom. Already a published poet, she had proved herself to a much wider audience with two well-received novels. Although the novels were very different in their subjects and their tone, they both came from essential aspects of Alvarez's life—her experiences as an immigrant and her country's painful history. With growing confidence, she could now move on to whatever subjects, styles, and genres she preferred.

Chapter 4

"My Bilingual, Bicultural Self"

Although she was now a novelist, Alvarez had not left poetry behind. She still considered it her first love. She also hoped that her popularity as a novelist might inspire some of her readers to pick up her poetry. In the United States and in the world at large, appreciation was now growing for writing that crossed borders of ethnicity and experience. With this in mind, Alvarez published her second collection of poetry in 1995. It was called *The Other Side/El Otro Lado*. Despite the collection's bilingual title, all the poems were in English. Alvarez did, however, sprinkle Spanish words freely throughout.

One of the poems in the collection, "Bilingual Sestina," again pays tribute to the maids who helped to bring up Alvarez in the Dominican Republic. She recalls how they taught her many of her first words. The poem acknowledges both the hardships and the advantages of having to learn English and becoming bilingual.

Other poems in *The Other Side/El Otro Lado*, such as the sequence called "The Joe Poems," explore the difficulties of relationships. The title poem, in twenty-one parts, is based on Alvarez's experience of living and writing at Altos de Chavón, the artists' colony in the Dominican Republic. The poem begins with a look at the other artists in the colony before moving out into a small Dominican town.

Homecoming Again

Shortly after *The Other Side/El Otro Lado* was published, Alvarez also revisited her first collection, *Homecoming*. It was reissued by Plume in 1996. The new edition was not simply a reprint, however. To reflect changes in her life and her state of mind, Alvarez made small changes to some of the original poems, and she added new poems. The sequence "33" had originally contained thirty-three sonnets, reflecting her age when *Homecoming* was first published. With thirteen additional sonnets, the sequence now contained forty-six poems, for Alvarez's age at the time the new edition was published.

Alvarez also commented that she wanted to give her younger self more of a Hispanic voice than she had originally dared to reveal. "In trying to find the voice that the speaker of '33' so anxiously searches for, I could not admit the further confusions of my bilingual, bicultural self," she wrote in the afterword to the revised version. "[In the new edition], I allowed that young Latina her little bits of Spanish, a *tía* here, a *Mami* there."[66]

"Mapping a Country That's Not on the Map"

While reflecting on her previous work and looking forward to new projects, Alvarez received an increasing number of honors, especially from her peers in the literary community. One exhibition placed her work alongside that of some of the greatest writers of all time. From December 1995 to April 1996 the New York Public Library ran an exhibition called "The Hand of the Poet: Original Manuscripts by 100 Masters, from John Donne to Julia Alvarez."

A consequence of Alvarez's increasing popularity and recognition by other writers was that both America and the Dominican Republic wanted to claim her as their own. Alvarez remembers being invited to speak at a meeting of the Caribbean Studies

From 2005 to 2006, Alvarez's work was included in an exhibit at the New York Public Library reading room. The exhibit featured original manuscripts by one hundred literary masters.

Association in Santo Domingo. Another speaker at the meeting was Aída Cartagena Portalatín, a Dominican poet famous in her own country but not especially well known abroad. Much to her surprise, Alvarez received a scolding in Spanish from Portalatín. "It doesn't seem possible," the old writer told Alvarez, "that a Dominican should write in English. Come back to your country, to your language. You are a Dominican."[67]

Not wanting to be rude, and not knowing how to answer, Alvarez said nothing to Portalatín. However, she had strong feelings about her own identity as a writer and as a woman. In fact, she felt so strongly about the matter that she later wrote an essay, "Doña Aída, with Your Permission," in response to Portalatín's remarks. "I am *not* a Dominican writer. I have no business writing in a language that I can speak but have not studied deeply enough to craft," Alvarez says in her essay. "But, you're right, Doña Aída, I'm also not una norteamericana. . . . That's why I describe myself as a Dominican American writer. That's not just a term. I'm mapping a country that's not on the map, and that's why I'm trying to put it down on paper."[68]

A Dominican in Vermont

Portalatín's complaint notwithstanding, Alvarez had found a home among the green fields and mountains of Vermont. Many now ranked her among the state's most distinguished literary luminaries. Alvarez was touched by the idea that she belonged to Vermont, but she also resisted it. After a lifetime of not belonging anywhere except for the homeland of the written word, she could not define herself by the place in which she lived. But she started to accept the idea that she could be "from" more than one place.

"What makes me lay the deepest claim to Vermont as my home state is that this is where I've written most of my books,"[69] she acknowledges. The tranquillity of Vermont, in the context of her happy marriage, made it a place where Alvarez could feel at home and be a productive writer.

Middlebury College also wanted to claim Alvarez. In 1996 the college promoted her to the position of full professor, five years after she was granted tenure. Alvarez had mixed feelings about the increased responsibilities of her position as a teacher. "My sister has a little restaurant, and I used to complain to her about

Professional Changes

In 1996 Alvarez was finally appointed as a full professor at Middlebury College, five years after being granted tenure. Just two years later, in 1998, she gave up her professorship to become Middlebury's writer-in-residence. Although many of her friends questioned her decision, after so many years in the teaching profession Alvarez wanted to devote more time to writing. As writer-in-residence, she could also maintain her connection to Middlebury.

Alvarez considers herself a "Dominican American writer," and she lives in the peaceful countryside of Vermont.

grading papers," she recalls. "I love the classroom, but grading all those stacks! She pointed out that every job has parts you don't like, 'I don't like to chop vegetables.'"[70]

In the meantime, another novel was in the works. While foreign-language editions of her books were appearing around the world—including Spanish translations for the Dominican Republic and Latin America—Alvarez came out with a sequel to *How the García Girls Lost Their Accents.*

"Fiction Tells the Truth"

The new novel, *¡Yo!* appeared in 1997. Even in its title, Alvarez was playing with some of her deepest fascinations, such as language and identity. *Yo* means "I" in Spanish, but the title also refers to Yolanda García, one of the sisters Alvarez had already written about so insightfully. At the start of *¡Yo!* Yolanda has become a published writer—and managed to alienate her family by writing a book that seems to be based on them. Once again, Alvarez was taking some inspiration from her own experiences.

Ironically, despite the meaning of the Spanish word *yo*, Yo García does not tell her own story. Part of the point of the novel, Alvarez explains, is to allow the people around the writer to express themselves about her and her work. The chapters have titles such as "The Mother," "The Landlady," and "The Third Husband." Each of these characters fills in his or her own section of the narrative. As in *García Girls*, each chapter is self-contained, but the chapters are all connected by their characters and themes to make up an entire story.

One chapter, "The Suitor," was later made into a film and shown on PBS stations in the United States. At this point in the story, Yo returns to the Dominican Republic for the summer, leaving her American boyfriend, Dexter Hays, behind. Dexter misses her so much that he follows her to the Dominican Republic, but he soon discovers that an American relationship is not the same in a foreign country. He is surrounded by his girlfriend's suspicious family, and the changed setting for their love only reminds both Yo and Dexter that they come from very different backgrounds. As difficult as she finds her family, Yo cannot detach herself from them as Dexter has done from his. "I couldn't live that way," she tells him. "I couldn't understand myself without the rest of the clan to tell me who I am."[71] In this comment from her main character, Alvarez insightfully captures one of the paradoxes of the book: We need to move away from our upbringing and define ourselves as individuals, but we also need others to remind us of who we are.

It was easy for some readers to assume that *¡Yo!* was straight autobiography, or almost. In some ways the new novel seemed even closer to Alvarez's experiences than had *García Girls*, because the central character had become a writer. Still, Alvarez explains in an interview that it was not that simple. "I write about the people whom we are going to find out about—the yo, or I," she said. "Of course, Yo is a part of me, but she is not me. . . . I feel that fiction tells the truth more than the facts do. . . . These creations come out of your experience, what you have read, what you are really interested in."[72]

Writer-in-Residence

Despite the stability that Alvarez had found with her husband and friends in Vermont, and despite her entry into the community of established writers, change was still a constant in her life. Since she had become a full professor at Middlebury College, her teaching had made increased demands on her time and energy. For Alvarez, the solution was to give up tenure and to continue teaching only on a part-time basis. In 1998 she resigned as a professor and became the writer-in-residence in Middlebury's English department.

"They won't let you keep tenure at Middlebury unless you teach full-time," she explains. "All my life I've been a teacher who writes on the side and now I am a writer who teaches on the side. It was terrifying, are you kidding? To say to myself, I am going to stretch my wings, I'm a writer, and do that."[73] Even as an established writer, Alvarez found herself missing the stability of full-time employment. But she welcomed the opportunity to throw herself wholeheartedly into her work, while not having to feel that she might be short-changing her students.

As writer-in-residence at Middlebury, Alvarez was able to maintain her strong connection to the college, which had been part of her life for so many years. She could still use the library for her own research and interests. Alvarez also continued to teach creative writing, and she assisted graduate students with their work. She became an adviser to Alianza Latinoamericana y Caribeña, the Latino student association at Middlebury. In appreciation of her efforts on their behalf, the Alianza students called her their *madrina*, or godmother. She felt a particular connection to the Dominican students. Some of them faced challenges, including an unfamiliar language, similar to those she and her family had endured when they arrived in the United States.

Writer and Activist

"When she's in Vermont, she can write and spin the stories she has inside. When she goes to the Dominican Republic, she can do things and be sort of that activist self that's been in there for awhile, but not really out."

—Patricia Lopez, quoted in Kerri Miller, "Author Julia Alvarez Thrives in Two Worlds," Minnesota Public Radio, 2007. www.minnesota.publicradio.org. [It appears Lopez was interviewed for the MPR piece.]

Somewhat surprisingly, Alvarez's first published work after giving up tenure was not another work of fiction. Instead, she felt that it was now time to reveal something more of herself to her readers through the medium of nonfiction.

Declaring Herself

Something to Declare, published in 1998, represented both a step forward for Alvarez and a rummage through her archives. It is a book of essays. These short pieces deal with wide-ranging topics, including her formative experiences while growing up in the Dominican Republic and in New York, her decision not to have children, and her habits and philosophies as a writer. Most of the essays had been written in the 1990s. Some of them had already been published in anthologies and magazines such as *Allure* and *Washington Post Magazine*.

However, the book is not just a random collection of Alvarez's writings. It is divided into two sections. The first section concentrates on Alvarez's background, family, and personal life, while the second is about her life as a writer. In the foreword to *Something to Declare*, Alvarez explains that she had started writing essays partly as a response to readers who wrote to her, asking for more information about her and her work. Sometimes she had intended

Alvarez gave a literary portrait of herself as a woman and as a writer in her book Something to Declare, *published in 1998.*

only to write a short letter, which then turned into something much longer and more involved. "That is the pretext of essays," she says in the foreword: *we have something to declare.*[74]

Several years later, Alvarez still felt that the portrait of herself as a woman and as a writer in *Something to Declare* was accurate. "I haven't changed my mind all that much since 1998 when it was published," she says, "which is kind of gratifying, to think that certain things remain true."[75]

Honors and Obligations

Alvarez's decision to become a writer first and foremost, rather than a teacher, was reinforced by another important honor from the literary establishment in 1999. New York librarians picked *How the García Girls Lost Their Accents* as one of twenty-one classic books that would continue to be read in the twenty-first century. The list also included such famous works as Anne Frank's *Diary of a Young Girl* and Gabriel García Márquez's *One Hundred Years of Solitude*.

The business of writing, like that of being a full-time teacher, brought its own obligations. Alvarez was not fond of the promotional requirements of the publishing industry. "The market develops an appetite for seeing the authors, hearing them on radio and television," she told an interviewer. "And in some ways that's a good thing. It gets the word out. That's why we authors do it. But in some ways often it becomes the thing that drives."[76] Alvarez noted that some people who attended her readings had never bothered to read any of her books.

Still, Alvarez realized that because of the success of her books, she could not completely avoid being a literary celebrity. Although she did not enjoy self-promotion, the accolades and attention her work garnered were not unwelcome. In 2000 a couple of significant honors came her way. The White House asked Alvarez to be part of a U.S. delegation to the inauguration of the Dominican Republic's new president, Hipólito Mejía, in August. In September *Latina* magazine named Alvarez its Woman of the Year. Such recognition was especially meaningful to Alvarez because it acknowledged both the Dominican and the American aspects of her background.

Dominican Republic president Hipólito Mejía speaks at the United Nations in 2004. Alvarez was asked by the White House to be part of a U.S. delegation at his inauguration.

Salomé and Camila

Alvarez's next novel, *In the Name of Salomé*, came out in 2000. However, Alvarez acknowledged that she had started research and work on it not long after finishing *In the Time of the Butterflies*. As was often the case in Alvarez's writing, the work she did on one book led her to a somewhat related topic in the next. *In the Name of Salomé* is another novel about real-life Dominican women who break away from the constraints of their time and status to achieve something of lasting importance.

The novel's title character is Salomé Ureña de Henríquez, a nineteenth-century Dominican poet and political activist. "I initially became interested in the life of this woman, Salome," Alvarez claims, "because here she was the first person ever to win a national medal in poetry in a country where machismo is STILL rampant."[77] *In the Name of Salomé* is also about Camila Ureña, Salomé's daughter. In alternating chapters, Alvarez unfolds both Salomé's and Camila's stories.

Part of the novel's interest lies in the fact that the two women are so different. Salomé died of tuberculosis when her daughter was only three years old, meaning that she was more of a legendary figure for Camila than a remembered parent. Camila left for Cuba with her father when Trujillo came to power. Trained as a teacher, she later went to the United States but eventually returned to Cuba. Alvarez portrays Camila as cautious and withdrawn, unlike her mother. However, both Salomé and Camila

A Visit to Cuba

Although Americans are seldom able to travel to Cuba, Alvarez and her husband were given special permission to go while she was researching *In the Name of Salomé*. In Cuba they visited the National Archives. Alvarez also met with the historian Ricardo Repilado, who gave her a valuable edition of Salomé Ureña de Henríquez's poems.

face racism and other forms of prejudice. Camila's efforts to organize Salomé's papers lead her to new discoveries about her mother and to a greater understanding of herself.

As part of her research for the novel, Alvarez wanted to visit Cuba, whose National Archives contains valuable artifacts from the lives of Camila and Salomé, including original letters and poems. Because the U.S. government has long restricted travel by its citizens to Cuba, however, Alvarez and her husband—who wanted to take photos to aid in the research—had to apply for permission to visit the country. Fortunately, that permission was granted, and Alvarez was able to examine the treasures in the National Archive.

Alvarez was also fortunate enough to meet someone who had known Camila personally. Ricardo Repilado, the city historian in Santiago de Cuba, agreed to meet with her and share his knowledge. Repilado gave her a rare 1920 edition of Salomé's poems. "I felt so moved but I didn't want to take it," Alvarez revealed.

> In a country that has so little of everything, including books, that he would give me that—I felt I couldn't take that. He said "I am an old man"—he's in his eighties—"I am going to die soon and there is no one around that I can leave this book to who will appreciate it as much as you. So take it with you." It was sitting here next to my computer as I worked as a kind of talisman.[78]

When *In the Name of Salomé* was published, it received some of the best reviews of Alvarez's career. Some reviewers drew special attention to the way that the novel brought out the connections between the political turmoil and the human emotions of two different centuries.

"Not Seeing Our Commonality"

Although proud to call herself Dominican American, Alvarez found herself constantly reassessing the implications of classifying ourselves by our national or ethnic backgrounds. This was especially the case after the horrifying events of September 11, 2001, when thousands died in terrorist attacks on American soil. "I'm frightened by a tendency for all of us to get ourselves into

The horror of the 9/11 terrorist attacks on the United States influenced Alvarez's writings.

our ethnic and racial bunkers and to separate ourselves from each other,"[79] she said in a post-9/11 interview for Hispanic Heritage Month.

When Alvarez learned of the attacks on the World Trade Center, her first thoughts were about the many Latinos and Dominicans who had died there. A friend pointed out that the tragedy of 9/11 was not about how many people of a certain nationality had died; they were all human beings. "I've gotten into this frame of mind, into this way of thinking that says what happened to my people, and that's precisely the kind of mentality that causes a 9/11, not seeing our commonality,"[80] she observed ruefully.

In her work Alvarez remained committed to a cross-cultural perspective that did, in fact, reflect the commonality of human experience. And by the start of the twenty-first century she had begun bringing that perspective to a different audience: younger readers.

A New Audience

Alvarez's first book for children, *The Secret Footprints*, was published in 2000. It is a beautifully illustrated picture book based on a Dominican legend. The creatures in the book, called *ciguapas*, resemble human beings, but they live in the sea. Because their feet are on backward, any footprints they leave on the beach as they emerge from the water make it look as if they are walking into the waves.

In 2001 *How Tía Lola Came to ~~Visit~~ Stay* was published. This book, for slightly older children, tells the story of a child whose Dominican parents get divorced, forcing him to move from New York to Vermont. There, he and his mother are joined by his eccentric aunt from the Dominican Republic. Although Alvarez was an adult when she moved to Vermont, she was again writing about what she knew—being uprooted as a child, living in the big city, and moving to a semirural community.

Alvarez's third book for younger readers, *Before We Were Free*, came out in 2002. This time, teenagers and young adults were the target audience. Though in structure and style it is less complex than Alvarez's adult books, *Before We Were Free* is considered by many to be one of her most important works. It revisits Trujillo's dictatorship, his downfall, and the aftermath—subjects that continued to preoccupy Alvarez even though she had treated them in depth in *In the Time of the Butterflies*.

Revisiting the Dictatorship

Before We Were Free is the story of Anita de la Torre, who is on the cusp of her teen years and whose family is caught up in the attempt to overthrow Trujillo. In some ways Alvarez based the book on her own family's experiences. She called the process of writing the book "a composite both of doing research and of remembering family stories."[81] The Garcías, who starred in *How the García Girls Lost Their Accents* and *¡Yo!* appear briefly at the beginning and the end. They are Anita's cousins, leaving for the safety of New York. Although the story is not biography or autobiography, the García family resembles the Alvarez family. There are parallels between Anita's family and some of Alvarez's relatives, who stayed behind and continued fighting against Trujillo. "I know I feel a special commitment to those who stayed behind in my native country, fighting for freedom and opportunities,"[82] Alvarez says.

Giving Thanks

"What is it with you Latinas and thank yous? Every Latina writer I read has at least a page of acknowledgments. You're all so polite!"

—Quoted in Julia Alvarez, "We Need to Understand," *Children and Libraries: The Journal of the Association for Library Service to Children*, vol.2, no. 2, Summer/Fall 2004, pp. 13–16.

In the course of the novel, Anita goes through some normal experiences for a twelve-year-old girl: first love, menstruation, writing in her diary. But the events that she writes about become increasingly frightening and tragic. Targeted by Trujillo's agents for their family's involvement in the underground movement against the dictator, Anita and her mother eventually go into hiding. Her father and uncle are thrown into prison, their future uncertain. Part of the novel's poignancy lies in the collision between a twelve-year-old's normal feelings and experiences and the unusual, terrifying situations that force her to grow up far too quickly. Both Anita's father and Chucha, her old nanny, tell her that she must eventually spread her wings and fly. "I guess I finally understand what she and Papi meant by wanting me to fly," Anita says near the end of the book. "To be free inside, like an uncaged bird. Then nothing, not even a dictatorship, can take away your liberty."[83]

Before We Were Free won the American Library Association's Pura Belpré Award for an exceptional children's book about the Latino experience. After winning the award, Alvarez wrote an essay called "We Need to Understand" in which she thanked those who had inspired the book and those who had recognized its achievement. She described her passion for the book's message:

> We have a tradition in Latin America of *el testimonio*, the testimony, bearing witness. The first step in the awakening of a people's fight for freedom is bearing witness, telling the story of where we have been in order to know where we are going. I wanted to bring young readers into that world of a dictatorship as seen from the eyes of another young person. I wanted young readers to experience firsthand the enormous cost of becoming a free person.[84]

Chapter 5

Steps Toward Saving the World

Alvarez has always had mixed feelings about her relationship with the Dominican Republic. Even though her earliest memories are of the tropical island where she grew up, it is very unlikely that she would have become a writer if her family had not left for the United States. In order to pursue her chosen career, Alvarez had to break free of her family's expectations for their Dominican daughter. She writes in English, not in Spanish, the language of her childhood. "And yet you're definitely writing out of a Dominican focus and background," she says about herself, "and maybe even a lot of your themes come from there, but it's another language and you've also gone through this other experience and sensibilities."[85] Although Alvarez is in some respects more American than Dominican, so much of her writing centers on the Dominican Republic that the country's profound influence on her is clear.

Since her books are so often set in the Dominican Republic, Alvarez would have liked to spend more time there, as a writer. But she is aware of the moral dilemma that this poses for her:

> If I could live part of the year and work in the Dominican
> Republic that would be great. . . . I love my homeland,

love being there, would love to do my deepest work there, i.e., writing. But when I'm there, I'm drawn into action because so much needs to be done. . . . No Medicaid. No unemployment. No teen pregnancy program. Writing feels like a luxury there, and that's a hard thing to come to terms with when you think of it as your calling."[86]

In 1996 Alvarez found a way to resolve some of her contradictory feelings about the Dominican Republic—in an unselfish way that would benefit the country. The Nature Conservancy, an environmental association, had asked Alvarez to contribute a story to an anthology it was producing. She and Eichner traveled to the Dominican Republic so that Alvarez could do research for that story. They visited the island's central mountain region, known for its production of delicious Dominican coffee. It was an area of her small country that Alvarez did not know well. She and Eichner were shocked by the condition of the land and its people. Although they were in an area of great natural beauty, large tracts of land had undergone clear-cutting so that more coffee could be produced. Alvarez also found that the coffee farmers were very poor. Many were being driven out of business by the major coffee companies.

"In the Dominican Republic, we've seen people paid as little as 33 cents a pound of coffee," says Alvarez. "They have to sell their plots because they can't make a living out of them. . . . The farmers go off to the urban centers where they can't get jobs, or they try to get illegally into the United States. It just starts a whole spiral."[87]

The Alta Gracia Farm

Alvarez, not inclined by nature to sit back and watch events unfold, wanted to do something to help these disadvantaged residents of her home country. This time, writing about what she saw might not be enough. With his farming background, Eichner, too, found himself deeply affected by the problems that the Dominican farmers faced. He had seen the decline of rural America and its farming communities. "His first love is farming," Alvarez says. "That's why we got involved."[88]

While doing research for a story in the Dominican Republic, Alvarez discovered that many coffee farmers were very poor and sometimes made only thirty-three cents per pound of coffee.

Julia Alvarez and her husband Bill Eichner purchased a coffee farm in the Dominican Republic named Alta Gracia. The farm creates jobs, and the workers are paid fair wages.

The local farmers knew that Alvarez and Eichner wanted to help them. Some of the farmers, unwilling to give up their traditional way of life without a fight, had formed a collective group and were trying to pool their resources. Working together, they hoped to keep their land and continue farming as they always had. The farmers asked Alvarez and Eichner to join the collective. Soon, the couple had purchased a farm in this isolated part of the Dominican Republic. They called it Alta Gracia, or "high grace." The farm's name came from *la Virgen de la Altagracia* (the Virgin of Altagracia), who is venerated in the Catholic Dominican Republic as a national patron saint. Alvarez has always thanked *la Virgen* in the dedications to her books.

Alta Gracia covers 260 acres (105ha) high in the mountains. The closest village, Los Marranitos, did not have electricity or running water when the couple bought the farm in 1996. Alvarez and Eichner were careful not to add to the scourge of deforestation. All of the coffee from Alta Gracia would be shade-grown (the traditional method) and organic, cultivated without using pesticides. A few other crops, including bananas and avocados, were introduced onto the farm. Alvarez and Eichner hired a small number of full-time employees. The farm also provided a lot of seasonal work for people living nearby, mainly when the coffee was ready for harvesting.

Alta Gracia's coffee is not cheap, but the higher prices mean that the people involved in the coffee's production can be paid more. The coffee is sold online through the farm's Web site, as well as in specialty stores in the United States. Because they are not spending much money on distribution or advertising, Alvarez and Eichner have ensured that the people working on the farm can be paid fairly.

Fundación Alta Gracia

While her husband worked on the details of running the farm, Alvarez pondered other ways to aid the community. Los Marranitos and the surrounding areas, she thought, could benefit from an increased cultural awareness. She considered turning part of Alta Gracia into an artists' retreat, somewhat like Altos de Chavón. Her friends and other artists could come to the farm and share their work with the local community.

After learning that 90 percent of the people living in and near Los Marranitos were illiterate, Alvarez established Fundación Alta Gracia, a literacy program that funds a school located on the farm.

However, Alvarez changed her ideas when she found out that more than 90 percent of the locals could not read or write. Without these basic skills, their options were greatly limited, and an arts center would not be of much benefit to them. It would be better, Alvarez decided, to establish a literacy program in the area. Although there was a school in Los Marranitos, neither the students nor the teacher spent much time there. From a practical perspective, the people of the village felt that their time was better spent in trying to earn as much money as possible. As a writer, Alvarez wanted to help the local people discover that their lives could expand in new and unexpected ways if they learned how to read and write.

The eventual result of Alvarez's ideas for a literacy program was Fundación Alta Gracia, which funds a school located on the farm. The school has thrived and helped the community through various initiatives. In 2000 a group of Middlebury College students visited Alta Gracia, dividing their time between working on the farm, teaching reading and writing to local residents, and working on their own creative writing projects.

By 2001 Alta Gracia had both a school and a library. That year Laura Marlow, a Middlebury graduate, became a volunteer teacher at Alta Gracia. Her students ranged in age from five to eighty-five. "If all that comes out of this is that people are able to say

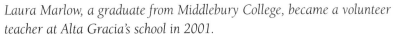

Laura Marlow, a graduate from Middlebury College, became a volunteer teacher at Alta Gracia's school in 2001.

the alphabet and recognize their names, that's a huge success,"[89] Marlow said.

Alvarez visits Alta Gracia as often as her schedule allows. While there, she finds herself doing anything from walking around the farm and looking over the crops with her husband, to conducting workshops and reading to local farmers and their children.

Writing for Younger Readers

Not surprisingly, the time that Alvarez spent among the mountains, the coffee plants, and people of her native country inspired more writing. *A Cafecito Story*, published in 2001, is the story of a farmer's son from Nebraska who visits the Dominican Republic. There, he spends time with a family growing organic coffee. Beautiful woodcuts by Belkis Ramírez, a well-known Dominican artist, illustrate the book. Eichner wrote an afterword about Alta Gracia and sustainable farming.

Increasingly, Alvarez was reading books for younger readers. Alta Gracia's library was full of children's books, because both the children and the adults in the local village were reading at a young person's level. Alvarez discovered classic children's books that she had never read in her own childhood, such as *Charlotte's Web* and *Pippi Longstocking*. This kind of reading led to books of hers such as *The Secret Footprints* and *Before We Were Free*.

In 2004 Alvarez published two more books for young readers, *Finding Miracles* and *A Gift of Gracias: The Legend of Altagracia*. *Finding Miracles*, a book for teenagers, deals with the experience of being an adopted child and searching for one's roots. Milly, a teenager living in Vermont, knows that she is adopted, but she has never been very curious about her birth family or her background. Then she meets Pablo, a student from a Latin American island nation. Although she is reluctant at first, Milly's friendship with Pablo leads her to travel to her birth country, finding adventures and miracles along the way. *A Gift of Gracias*, like *The Secret Footprints*, is a picture book. The story's miraculous events are inspired by the Virgin of Altagracia.

Alvarez also published a poetry collection, *The Woman I Kept to Myself*, in 2004. The years since she gave up tenure at Middlebury and started the Alta Gracia farm with her husband have been some of her most prolific and rewarding.

At Alta Gracia's library, Alvarez discovered classic children's books such as Charlotte's Web. *These stories began to influence her own writing.*

Trying to Save the World

Saving the World, Alvarez's 2006 novel, brought her back to writing for an adult audience. This book grew out of the increasing amount of time that Alvarez was spending in the Dominican Republic and also out of a minor piece of information that she had come across while writing *In the Name of Salomé*.

In late 1803 the king of Spain dispatched a court physician, Francisco Xavier Balmis, on an extraordinary mission: to spread a recently discovered smallpox vaccine around the world. At the time, smallpox was a devastating disease. The smallpox virus was easily passed from person to person, and it was highly lethal. Victims fortunate enough to survive were often left disfigured.

Balmis set sail with a medical team and twenty-two orphan boys. The vaccine consisted of a live—but nonlethal—pox virus. Because refrigeration was not available in the early nineteenth century, the vaccine virus had to be transported by human hosts. The orphan boys were used as these hosts.

A Shining Light

"Whatever the topic, Senora Alvarez's wit, intelligence, and compassion shine through."

—Robert Birnbaum, "Interviews: Julia Alvarez," 2006. www.identitytheory.com.

By 1804, when Balmis's expedition reached the Americas, the island of Hispaniola—where the Dominican Republic and Haiti are located—was in the midst of a smallpox outbreak. But Hispaniola was also in the middle of a bloody revolution, as the island's inhabitants struggled to free themselves from French rule. Because of the fighting, the expedition did not stop on Hispaniola. Its people were, therefore, unable to benefit from the precious vaccine, which had been brought across the ocean by its young human carriers.

Alvarez was intrigued by this historical footnote. Although the story was inspiring, she also found it ironic that the boys had little or no choice in the matter. "Though the Spanish crown's motives were praised as noble, I could not stop thinking of those twenty-two boys," she recalls. "Must civilization *always* ride on the backs of those least able to defend themselves? Little boys! Orphans!"[90]

As in most of her books, a strong female character—and then two—made her way into the story. The orphanage's religious guardian, Doña Isabel, was the only woman who joined the expedition. Her main duty was to look after the boys, but she also got caught up in the ambitions and power struggles of the men involved.

Alvarez wanted to experience some of what Isabel had gone through. So she spent time on a sailing ship, *Spirit of Massachusetts*, where she found out for herself what it felt like to be seasick. She also went to La Coruña, the port in northwest Spain from where the expedition had set out. There, she climbed the

Alvarez's novel Saving the World *focuses on Francisco Xavier Balmis, who tried to spread the recently discovered smallpox vaccine around the world in the early 1800s.*

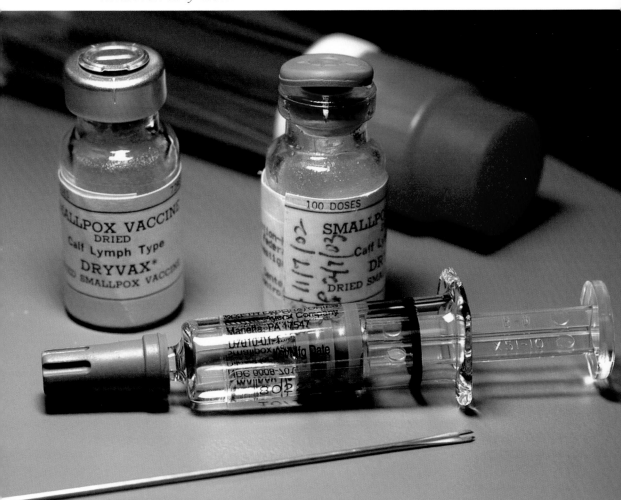

Inspired by True Events

Initially, Alvarez intended to set her novel *Saving the World* entirely in the nineteenth century. However, after the terrible events of September 11, 2001, she decided that she needed to make the story of the Spanish smallpox expedition more relevant to the twenty-first century.

Tower of Hercules, the oldest functioning Roman lighthouse in the world. "It had beamed a good-bye to the rectoress and her twenty-two boys,"[91] she recalls. In Madrid, Alvarez met Catherine Mark, an American who was an expert on Balmis and his expedition. In addition to sharing what she knew, Mark put Alvarez in touch with other people around the world who could fill in parts of the story.

Originally, *Saving the World* was set entirely in the nineteenth century, exploring the events of the smallpox vaccine expedition. After the terrorist attacks of September 11, 2001, however, Alvarez wanted to make the novel relevant in the new millennium. "Like many Americans, I was shaken up" by the attacks, she said.

> I wanted to bring the story of the expedition forward into my own time. What can stories do for us when we are muddling through difficulties in our own lives? Does it matter that we know the stories of the past before we, too, become history? How do we keep faith with what is grand? And so I created a writer, Alma, going through her own dark night of the soul.[92]

Like Alvarez, Alma is a Dominican American writer, living in Vermont. Her husband travels to the Dominican Republic to work on environmental issues and AIDS research. While there, he is captured by guerrillas as Alma faces other challenges and tragedies at home. Although Alma's and Isabel's stories may seem very different, many parallels emerge in the course of the book.

As in her previous novel *In the Name of Salomé*, Alvarez shifts back and forth between the two stories and the two women's perspectives. "These two stories, seemingly so different, begin to 'speak' to each other," she explains, "and I hope there is, if not a full rhyme, then a sort of half-rhyme: a hope that stories can make a difference in a world that increasingly seems beyond any kind of redemption."[93]

"My Life Took a Different Turn"

In her own life, Alvarez continues to be every bit as dynamic as her characters. In the United States and the Dominican Republic, she is highly visible as an author and as an activist for social change. In 2006, for example, while promoting *Saving the World*, she appeared at the Los Angeles Book Festival with about 350 other writers. Not content simply to discuss her work and to spend time with other writers, she also joined a street rally in support of undocumented immigrants.

Finding Inspiration

"Virtually all of her work is centered in or springs from the Dominican Republic. Its culture, its attitudes, folktales, stories, the class differences—everything, it's all reflected through the whole body of her writing."

—Patricia Lopez, quoted in Kerri Miller, "Author Julia Alvarez Thrives in Two Worlds," Minnesota Public Radio, 2007. minnesota.publicradio.org.

She began working on a nonfiction book about a unique tradition in Hispanic culture: the *quinceañera* parties for Latina girls on their fifteenth birthday. These parties are often very lavish, and many families of humble means go deeply into debt to pay for them. "Imagine, a whole community spends three months, six, a year, preparing and focusing on its young girls," Alvarez said of *quinceañeras*. "Quite an investment of time and energy, and it makes the girls feel supported, loved, encouraged to be the new up and coming leaders in the community."[94] Alvarez's book, which also examines the growing Latino community in the United States, was scheduled to appear in the summer of

2007 under the title *Once Upon a Quinceañera: Coming of Age in the U.S.A.*

As a writer, Julia Alvarez has produced an impressive body of work, from poetry and novels to autobiography and children's literature. Although she has embraced her Dominican American identity and is seen as an inspiration to Latinos and women particularly, Alvarez has touched readers from a wide variety of countries and backgrounds.

Alvarez also wrote nonfiction books about Hispanic traditions such as the quinceañera, a party that is held for a girl when she turns fifteen.

"I don't think I have more integrity or spirituality than anybody else in my family," she says. "It's just that my life took a different turn. We came to this country and here I became one of the others."[95] Becoming an immigrant, one of "the others," set Alvarez free to become aware of those who are unlike herself. Although a proud Hispanic American, she is truly an author without borders, taking herself and her readers into the homeland of the written word.

Notes

Introduction: A Universal Voice

1. Walsh, Elsa, "Arms and the Women," *Washington Post Book World*, November 27, 1994, p. 7.

2. Julia Alvarez, "About Me." www.juliaalvarez.com/about.

3. Julia Alvarez, interview by Robert Birnbaum, "Author Interviews," *identitytheory.com*, May 22, 2006. www.identitytheory.com/interviews/birnbaum171.php.

4. Julia Alvarez, *Something to Declare*. New York: Plume, 1998, p. 169.

5. Alvarez, interview by Birnbaum.

6. Alvarez, *Something to Declare*, p. 129.

Chapter 1: The Dominican American Child

7. Alvarez, *Something to Declare*, p. 7.

8. Alvarez, *Something to Declare*, p. 3.

9. Alvarez, *Something to Declare*, p. 106.

10. Selden Rodman, *Quisqueya: A History of the Dominican Republic*. Seattle: University of Washington Press, 1964, p. 146.

11. Alvarez, *Something to Declare*, p. 149.

12. Alvarez, *Something to Declare*, p. 155.

13. Julia Alvarez, "I, Too, Sing América." Writers on America— Office of International Information Programs, U.S. Department of State. http://usinfo.state.gov/products/pubs/writers/alvarez.htm.

14. Quoted in Dwight Garner, "Something to Declare," *Salon.com*, 2000, p. 1. www.salon.com/mwt/feature/1998/09/25feature. html.

15. Alvarez, *Something to Declare*, p. 145.

16. Alvarez, *Something to Declare*, p. 105.

17. Quoted in Garner, "Something to Declare," p. 3.

18. Alvarez, *Something to Declare*, p. 17.

19. Julia Alvarez, interview by Barnes & Noble.com, *"Before We Were Free*: Interviews and Essays." http://search.barnesand noble.com/booksearch/isbninquiry.asp?ean=9780440237846 &displayonly=ITV&z=y#ITV.

20. Quoted in Marcela Valdes, "The Reluctant Celebrity," *Publishers Weekly*, March 27, 2006, p. 2.

21. Alvarez, *Something to Declare*, p. 140.

22. Alvarez, *Something to Declare*, p. 158.

23. Quoted in Thomson Gale, "Hispanic Heritage: Julia Alvarez," 2007. www.gale.com/free_resources/chh/bio/alvarez_j.htm.

Chapter 2: Learning Her Craft

24. Alvarez, *Something to Declare*, p. 62.

25. Julia Alvarez, interview by Bookreporter.com, "Author: Julia Alvarez," September 22, 2000. www.bookreporter.com/ authors/au-alvarez-julia.asp.

26. Alvarez, *Something to Declare*, p. 160.

27. Alvarez, interview by Birnbaum.

28. Alvarez, *Something to Declare*, p. 66.

29. Julia Alvarez, interview by Karla Davis, "Julia Alvarez Discusses the Experience of Emigrating to America and How Her Views on Identity Have Changed Since September 11," transcript, *All Things Considered*, September 15, 2002, p. 2.

30. William Carlos Williams, *Selected Poems*. New York: New Directions, 1985, p. 56.

31. Alvarez, *Something to Declare*, p. 164.

32. Alvarez, interview by Bookreporter.com, p. 8.

33. Julia Alvarez, online interview by Barnes & Noble.com, May 26, 1998. http://search.barnesandnoble.com/booksearch/isb ninquiry.asp?ean=9780452279186&displayonly=ITV&z=y#ITV.

34. Alvarez, *Something to Declare*, p. 216.

35. Alvarez, *Something to Declare*, p. 220.

36. Alvarez, interview by Birnbaum, p. 10.

37. Alvarez, *Something to Declare*, p. 222.

38. Alvarez, *Something to Declare*, p. 179.

39. Alvarez, interview by Bookreporter.com.

40. Alvarez, *Something to Declare*, p. 161.

41. Julia Alvarez, *Homecoming: New and Collected Poems*. New York: Plume, 1996, p. 118.

42. Alvarez, *Homecoming*, p. 9.

43. Pamela White Hadas, "Julia Alvarez: *Homecoming*," Faculty Bookshelf, Middlebury College. www.middlebury.edu/acad emics/ump/majors/english/bookshelf/alvarez/homecoming.htm.

Chapter 3: García Girls and Butterflies

44. Quoted in Valdes, "The Reluctant Celebrity," p. 1.

45. Quoted in Garner, "Something to Declare," p. 4.

46. Alvarez, *Something to Declare*, p. 190.

47. Alvarez, *Something to Declare*, 89.

48. Alvarez, "I, Too, Sing América," p. 4.

49. Julia Alvarez, online interview by Barnes & Noble.com, "Books: *Yo!*" p. 2. http://search.barnesandnoble.com/book search/isbninquiry.asp?ean=9780452279186&displayonly=IT V&z=y#ITV.

50. Julia Alvarez, *How the García Girls Lost Their Accents*. New York: Plume, 1991, p. 138.

51. Quoted in Alvarez, *García Girls*, p. iii.

52. Quoted in Alvarez, *García Girls*, p. i.

53. Alvarez, *Something to Declare*, p. 125.

54. Alvarez, *Something to Declare*, p. 198.

55. Alvarez, *Something to Declare*, p. 200.

56. Alvarez, *Something to Declare*, p. 209.

57. Julia Alvarez, *In the Time of the Butterflies*. New York: Plume, 1994, p. 324.

58. Alvarez, *Something to Declare*, p. 273.

59. Alvarez, *Butterflies*, p. 253.

60. Andrea Schaefer, "Julia Alvarez," in *American Writers, Supplement VII*, Jay Parini ed. New York: Charles Scribner's Sons, 2001, p. 13.

61. Quoted in Alvarez, *In the Time of the Butterflies*, p. ii.

62. Quoted in Alvarez, *In the Time of the Butterflies*, p. iii.

63. Julia Alvarez, interview by Powells.com, "Ink Q&A," 2006. www.powells.com/ink/alvarez.html.

64. Alvarez, *Something to Declare*, p. 111.

65. Alvarez, interview by Birnbaum.

Chapter 4: "My Bilingual, Bicultural Self"

66. Alvarez, *Homecoming*, p. 119.

67. Alvarez, *Something to Declare*, p. 171.

68. Alvarez, *Something to Declare*, pp. 172–73.

69. Alvarez, "*Something to Declare*, p. 190.

70. Alvarez, interview by Birnbaum.

71. Julia Alvarez, *¡Yo!* New York: Plume, 1997, p. 209.

72. Alvarez, online interview with Barnes & Noble.com.

73. Alvarez, interview by Bookreporter.com.

74. Alvarez, *Something to Declare*, p. xiv.

75. Alvarez, "About Me."

76. Alvarez, interview by Birnbaum.

77. Alvarez, interview by Bookreporter.com.

78. Alvarez, interview by Bookreporter.com.

79. Alvarez, interview by Davis, p. 1.

80. Alvarez, interview by Davis, p. 1.

81. Alvarez, interview by Barnes & Noble.com.

82. Alvarez, interview by Barnes & Noble.com.

83. Julia Alvarez, *Before We Were Free*. New York: Alfred A. Knopf, 2002, p. 160.

84. Julia Alvarez, "We Need to Understand," *Children and Libraries: The Journal of the Association for Library Service to Children*, Summer/Fall 2004, p. 16.

Chapter 5: Steps Toward Saving the World

85. Quoted in Garner, "Something to Declare," p. 2.

86. Alvarez, interview by Powells.com.

87. Quoted in Valdes, "The Reluctant Celebrity," p. 2.

88. Alvarez, interview by Birnbaum, p. 10.

89. Quoted in Deborah Jones, "Alvarez Brews Up Coffee with a Social Conscience." *Middlebury Campus*, October 10, 2001, pp. 5–6.

90. Julia Alvarez, "La Ñapa," 2006. www.juliaalvarez.com/napa.

91. Alvarez, "La Ñapa."

92. Alvarez, "La Ñapa."

93. Alvarez, interview by Powells.com.

94. Alvarez, interview by Birnbaum, p. 22.

95. Alvarez, interview by Birnbaum, p. 17.

Important Dates

1950
Julia Alvarez is born on March 27 in New York City. A few months later, her family returns to the Dominican Republic.

1960
Her family immigrates to New York because of her father's underground activities against the dictator Trujillo.

1967–1969
Attends Connecticut College; attends the Bread Loaf School of English Writers' Conference during the summer of 1969.

1971
Graduates from Middlebury College, Vermont, with a Bachelor of Arts degree.

1975
Completes her Master of Fine Arts degree in creative writing at Syracuse University.

1979–1981
Teaches English at Phillips Academy Andover.

1984
Publishes her first poetry collection, *Homecoming*.

1988
Becomes an assistant professor of English at Middlebury College.

1989
Marries Bill Eichner, a doctor from Nebraska.

1991
Publishes her first novel, *How the García Girls Lost Their Accents*.

1994
Publishes *In the Time of the Butterflies*.

1996

With her husband, purchases the Alta Gracia farm in the Dominican Republic.

2000

Publishes *In the Name of Salomé*.

2002

Publishes *Before We Were Free*.

2006

Publishes *Saving the World*.

For More Information

Books

Julia Alvarez, *Before We Were Free*. New York: Alfred A. Knopf, 2002. A poignant tale for teens, this book deals with a girl growing up in the Dominican Republic during the brutal dictatorship of Rafael Trujillo.

————, *Finding Miracles*. New York: Alfred A. Knopf, 2004. In this novel for young adults, an adopted teenager searches for her roots.

————, *How the García Girls Lost Their Accents*. New York: Plume, 1991. Julia Alvarez's first novel deals with the trials and tribulations of four Dominican American sisters.

————, *In the Time of the Butterflies*. New York: Plume, 1994. This novel brought the tragic story of the Dominican Republic's Mirabal sisters to a large audience.

————, *Something to Declare*. New York: Plume, 1998. A collection of essays dealing with wide-ranging subjects, including love, family, the immigrant experience, and writing.

Web Sites

Altos de Chavón Cultural Center Foundation (www.altos dechavon.com). Julia Alvarez has taught at this Dominican educational and cultural institution. The Web site details the foundation's history, philosophy, and programs.

Café Alta Gracia (www.cafealtagracia.com). Finca Alta Gracia is a 60-acre (24-ha) coffee farm in the Dominican Republic that is owned by Julia Alvarez and her husband, Bill Eichner. This Web site provides information about the sustainable farming practices used at Alta Gracia, as well as the literacy program its profits support.

Hispaniola.com (www.hispaniola.com/dominican_republic/info). Provides basic information about the Dominican Republic, including its natural resources, history, and society.

Julia Alvarez (www.juliaalvarez.com). The official Web site of Julia Alvarez includes a short autobiographical sketch, the author's reflections on each of her books, a list of articles and interviews, and images.

Index

99

Picture Credits

About the Author

Clarissa Aykroyd is a graduate of the University of Victoria, Canada. She has published several books for younger readers on subjects as diverse as *Native American Horsemanship*, *Refugees*, and *Jonathan Swift*. Since leaving Victoria, where she grew up, she has lived in Dublin, Ireland, and currently lives in London, England.